A Middling Sense of Achievement

Obediah Bones

Archway Publishing books may be ordered through booksellers or by contacting:

Archway Publishing
1663 Liberty Drive
Bloomington, IN 47403
www.archwaypublishing.com
844-669-3957

ISBN: 978-1-6657-4061-6 (sc)
ISBN: 978-1-6657-4060-9 (e)

Library of Congress Control Number: 2023905031

Print information available on the last page.

Archway Publishing rev. date: 04/03/2023

Contents

I.   Birth

1.   Longing 2
2.   Wings 3
3.   Afternoon Showers 4
4.   Nobody 5
5.   Ecclesiastes 6
6.   Preacher's Pride 7
7.   Shepherd's Song 8
8.   Jonothan 9
9.   Growing Old 10
10. Let Them Play 11
11. Something 12
12. Human 13

II.   Death

13. Ghost 15
14. Old God/Hypocrite 16
15. Remember 17
16. Sobriety 18
17. Nickel and Nicotine 19
18. Silence 20
19. Ascending on a Horizontal Plane 21
20. How Long 23
21. Hard to Love 24
22. Death of a Poet 25
23. The Condemned Man's Lullaby 26
24. Forsake 28
25. Jawbone 29
26. Holy Grail 30
27. Garden 31

III.   Somewhere In Between

28. Flight 33
29. Early Morning 34

30.	Captain James Hook	35
31.	Working Class	36
32.	Barstools	37
33.	Alchemist	38
34.	Spit	39
35.	Jezebel	40
36.	Run Away	41
37.	A Travelling Song	42
38.	A Bit of Him	44
39.	Daydream IV: Dad Shoes	45
40.	Daydream III: Lovely	46
41.	Seasons	47
42.	A Romance of Shadows	48
43.	A Small Brown Spider	49
44.	Autumn Death	50
45.	Soon, We're Going Sailing, Brother	51
46.	Funny	52
47.	Darkness Dawning	53
48.	A Brief Lament	54
49.	Tapping	55
50.	Sailing	56
51.	Kissing	57
52.	Road Trips and Song Skips	58
53.	Home	59
54.	Chant	60
55.	Just One More Drive	62
56.	Lover, Sinner, Dancer, Brother, Sister	63
57.	Making Friends	64
58.	Another Song	65
59.	Far Far Down Below	67
60.	Rain	69
61.	Christmas	70
62.	Flirt	71
63.	Revel	72

I.
<u>Birth</u>

Longing

Why is love
Always spelled
Like longing?

Like when you
Introduced yourself
As Pain

And all I
Could say was
Don't leave me

Wings

One slipped throught the cracks
Of the human machine
But there's no going back
For we can't make it seem
We were wrong
Said God to the cherub

But we can't leave them there
In a world so cruel
Alone, shunned, and scared
A lost puppet, a fool
Were we wrong?
Said the cherub to God

Don't dare question my ways
I am right in all things
With his terrible gaze
God then neutered the wings
Of another who
Wondered too much

So the world moves on
See my glorious work
Nothing can stop my plan
God declared with a smirk
No moral or human
No angel or prayer
You are wrong
Said God to the cherub

Am I wrong?
Said the child who
Didn't have wings

Afternoon Showers

A moment's lapse in sanity
A goddess in the rain
I've always hated deity
Yet was drawn into your pain

Often I wonder where along
The way I sold my bread
To buy a soul that don't belong
With what's inside my head

So ask yourself the question
That begs you to be known
Sacrifice a bit of reason
Feel a little less alone

Nobody

Don't have to be good at hidin'
When nobody wants you found
Don't have to look like you're tryin'
If nobody's ever around

See, nobody's loyal
And nobody's kind
And nobody never will
Leave you behind
And nobody always is
Close by your side
And nobody ever stays
Long in my mind

Last night I was smokin' and thought I was dyin'
And nobody answered my call
And loneliness tickles the heart while it's dryin'
And nobody's there when you fall

Nobody's my friend
To nobody I pray
Nobody will notice
When I go away
And nobody follows
Even as I change
And everyone left me
But nobody stays

Ecclesiastes

Teach the kids early to feel unworthy
I learned my lessons well
Can I escape the unkillable weight
When heaven itself feels like hell

Justice is heavy but pity is deadly
Indifference walks easy and light
My memory dies to keep me alive
Till sorrow nests in for the night

Anger and misery beg you for company
Shame says you're better alone
Happiness flies when it leaves you behind
And blame wears you down to the bone

Give drug to the hurting and drink to the dying
When trying to live takes its toll
Take drugs cause I'm hurting and drink cause I'm dying
And nobody makes it out whole

Preacher's Pride

Lambkin, come back to the fold
You think you know what's right
How will you endure in the cold
Without the stained glass light

Lambkin, will you rest a while
Your way is long and bitter
Your anger dripping out like bile
To warm you in the winter

Lambkin, full of heresy
A broken will is what you need
So get down on your hands and knees
And mouth your prayers to me

Lambkin, you have gone astray
I will not ask you why
You've left the narrow holy way
To dance along the sky

Lambkin, you're no longer mine
You've gone too far to save
I'll never let you up to God
If you must always be so brave

Shepherd's Song

Ever dead and never dying
Empty sockets ever spying
Lipless, toothless, grinning, lying
Child, 'ware the Man of God

Swollen falsehoods, maggots teeming
Empty words and silent screaming
Rotting sweetness, hungry breathing
Child, spurn the Cup of God

Loathsome fingers, grasping, mauling
For coin or pleasure come they crawling
To rend from conscience soul and calling
Child, 'ware the Hand of God

The bed where shame makes tools of hate
Dread thirst the blood of serfs won't slake
None shall escape the sinner's fate
Child, flee the House of God

Walk not the paths nor streets of gold
Those narrow ways are not so old
Return to ancient field and fold
Dear Child, heed the Shepherd's Song

Jonothan

Jonothan
Rise from the brothers
Angel of death
Sweet breath of song

Jonothan
Some tall lanky kid
A gray haired woman
Asked if he was lost

Jonothan
Damned from birth
A living curse
Still too kind sometimes

Jonothan
Still a bit shy
Wit quick and smile dry
Can't sit still for too long

Jonothan
Poor child of mine
I brought you here
Just to survive

Jonothan
Someday we both will die
A pair of wings will rise
Of starkest grey
Of you and I

Growing Old

Fate don't need you

It won't ask twice

Will I grow old

Or roll the dice

When being young

Always has a price

Who ever got far

On good advice

Everything dies

Stuck in a cage

We all feel pain

What's really safe

So burn my bags

If you're gonna stay

Forget my face

As I'm running away

You'll never fly

If you can't let go

I'd ask, but I

Don't want to know

Fate don't need me

Won't ask again

As I grow old

On cold chagrin

Was being young

Just smoke and gin

Naivety

Or silent sin

I'm gonna die

Stuck with this face

When I'm in pain

I feel most safe

So burn my clothes

Forget my name

And don't look back

As I'm running away

You're gonna fly

No one can hold on

I'd ask, but I'm

Already gone

Let Them Play

When the world was small from the top of a tree
The pain that I knew was still smaller than me
And the loneliness hadn't yet set my heart free
Let him play, let him play, let him play

Before I discovered my love could be wrong
Before my shame haunted my bones like a song
And before the damned list of my sins grew so long
Let him play, let him play, let him play

They bought up my love and they sold it for water
And left me with nothing to say
Reached into my chest with a brand and a solder
Why didn't they just let him play?

Oh, how you did suffer, my curious child
The woods, they are not far away
I'll meet you there soon, when our time here is through
And we'll play, how we'll play, oh we'll play

As the blue winter wind scorches my lips again
A melancholy season of dry smoke and gin
Time to reclaim the ax from the kindling bin
Let him play, let him play, let him play

I've been lonesome enough for a decade or two
My feet have grown restless inside of these shoes
You sure don't need me and I don't damn need you
Let him play, let him play, let him play

The end of a childhood brings the same feeling
As the end of a storybook tale
You can't stop it no more than you stop time from stealing
As long as you can, let them play

Oh, how you did suffer, my curious child
The woods, they are not far away
I'll meet you there soon when our time here is through
And we'll play, how we'll play, oh we'll play

Something

There's something in the way you cry
With nothing in your eyes but tears
Your jawline set, your cheeks all wet
Your sadness locked away inside

There's something in the way you laugh
Like nothing matters anymore
Almost forget the losing bet
They carved into your epitaph

There's something in the way you smile
That always steals my gaze
Unknown intent, punishment set
I cannot know you undefiled

There's something in the way you think
When you and I have nothing left
We've lost our bets, I've no regrets
I'm drowning with you when we sink

Human

It's nearly there, but then it's gone
Some recognition in her eyes
She almost saw a human there
Before returning to her mind
I wonder what I am to her
And if it's more than half-assed lies

Another dozen passing by
Stuck glassy eyed in glowing screens
I barely see the people there
Just empty flesh fueled by machines
It's easy now to dissapear
When I am rarely even seen

I'm better off alone! I cry
The bastards barely care to glance
I smile to myself and shrug
To prove my point was worth the chance
I almost miss a pair of eyes
A brown so deep they seem to dance

A boy of two or maybe three
Before his mother pulls him on
He smiles at me wild and free
And then, just like the rest, he's gone
This thought will be the death of me
Maybe this world ain't quite so wrong

II.
<u>Death</u>

Ghost

There was something I forgot
I've known it for a while
The language never formed itself
In brew or blood or bile

I searched for god in forests old
In lips dyed cherry red
I found his corpse 'neath a small stone
And ground the bones for bread

Haunted by the ghost
Of the god my people killed
They say that he don't speak no more
Then why is my head filled
With longings of a cosmic kind
Unknown desires meld
Into my feeble mind they sink
Skull grey electric gel
I sliced my palms with sharpened nails
Communion red wine spilled
Haunted by the ghost
Of the god my people killed

It takes great weight to drag through hell
Hate draped in shame, a uranium gown
Melts flesh to fabric, silk to skin
The radiant light of purification

Step back and look at what you've created
Curse all of your prophets of self-validation
You call it all progress, all twisted and tainted
The red and the gold of your infatuation

Haunted by the ghost
Of the god my people killed
Sometimes I wonder why he died
'Twas us who birthed him too
Decimating innocents
On a crusade for truth
Is each of us the antichrist?
You dare to ask for proof?
The void I find in every thought
Swallows each thought like pills
Haunted by the ghost
Of the god my people killed

Old God/Hypocrite

Yes, your god still demands blood
Why do you think I have these scars?

◇◇◇

If happiness were a virtue
Then I would have been a saint
And yet you still judge me
For transgressing the very ideals
You hold as worthy
And neglect to observe for yourself

Remember

Remember when your voice had meaning
Now it's all just silent screaming
Choking on your hard-earned breathing
Purging blood with stainless steel
Cloud your thoughts with pain that's real

Remember when your words meant things
Before your fears began to sing
Calling broken hearts to cling
To splintered shards of memory
Drip ink from severed arteries

Remember when you knew my name
When life was just a boring game
When love and hate were not the same
Now cancer sells at dollar stores
And you can't help but pay for more

Remember when I thought I knew
The person who I thought was you
I'm thinking now it wasn't true
You never questioned what you did
Some things, my dear, I won't forgive

Sobriety

Floating past, nowhere fast
Mild high in your blue eyes
We sail out toward the moon
And when they ask you
Tell them that
We won't be back so soon

Bloody lips, lovers kiss
Suck the red all from my head
And dance me to my tomb
And when they ask you
Tell them that
I won't be back so soon

Broken plans, wedding bands
Stop the praise to meet my gaze
And give in to our doom
And when they ask me
I'll tell them
We won't be back so soon

Heavy scene, snort caffine
Chemicals and oval pills
Alone in a white room
And when you ask them
They'll tell you
I won't be back so soon

Doctor's note, winter coat
Discharged into March again
I'm scrubbing with a broom
Would you move on
If I told you
I won't be back so soon

Nickel and Nicotine

It's not the stained teeth
It's not the burnt lungs
For me
But when I burned a hole
In the t-shirt that you wore
The one I stole before
You left my heart hung from
A tree

I don't need to be pretty
I don't need to be wise
Or fine
But when I dance alone
With tears soaking my bones
I remember other homes
I knew in some short life
Of mine

It's not the white of wings
It's not the perfect lines
Of song
I do not crave another hell
And heaven still won't treat me well
There's little left for me to sell
Or pawn

Silence

It's been a while since I've said a word
At least a day or maybe more
And so I speak your name aloud
Remind me what I'm still here for

The inward road leads ever on
And thinking never stops the thoughts
I'd rather get to know you more
Your love is greater than my war
And wiser than the things that I have taught

There's little I can offer you, my dear
You steal my reason and my wit away
Just speak the word and I will stay right here
And give my all to love you, come what may

I hear you in the silence
And I see you in my dreams
Just say that you don't want me and
I'll fill my head with sound so I can sleep

Ascending on a Horizontal Plane

I got blood on my shoes
I got holes in my feet
I got a twin mattress
I got nowhere to sleep
I got three little words
That don't mean a thing
I got lyric confessions
I ain't never gon' sing

I got poisons for pleasure
Perscriptions for pain
Don't buy them from me
I'll get paid all the same
I got lost in my highschool
Couldn't tell if I'm sane
I can't question my teachers
It would ruin my grades

I saw a church sign
Said "Jesu kills shame"
I walked out with a gun
Seemed like a fair trade
I saw a young woman
Abused by her man
I said, Some don't get freedom
I learned that in 'Nam

Saw another young lady
A'speakin' her mind
I screamed, Know your place
And I burned her with fire
A cop pulled me over
As I's speedin' away
I said, She had it comin'
He said, Have a nice day

21

I got morals and rules
Lists that never grow smaller
So your Tower of Babel
Won't grow any taller
I got a big penthouse
The tallest there be
So look up for your Savior
It is I you will see

I'll meet God there first
When he comes floating down
He'll make me the President
Of my dear old home town

I will stand there in front of him
And shake his right hand
And then with his Almighty Strength
Finish my All-Knowing Plans

How Long

Chain the children
To a golden vice

          Late to the club
          On a Sunday night

                    Dragged through the streets
                      Like a sinners' christ

          How long, how long
          Must it be like this?

Call it a lie
If you don't want the truth

          Drown out the dying
          And drown out the proof

                    Fight through the war
                    Die on poverty's boot

          How long, how long
          Must it be like this?

Kill the dissenters
And call them insane

          Nothing to lose left
          And mammon to gain

                    Scrub away skin
                    Under warm acid rain

          How long, how long
          Must it be like this?

Inbred confusion
Breeds cannibal fear

          Whisper your sadness
          Where no one can hear

                    Sorrow sleeps heavy
                    'Neath blankets of tears

          How long, how long
          Must it be like this?

Hard to Love

Burning eyes and sleepless nights
Feels like my head's on fire
Heart strung out and mind in doubt
Crawling across a power wire

Burning sage, don't know my age
A fallen brother's cry
Hollow praise, salute the knaves
Who sent their boys to die

A racous sound, I hit the ground
Newly acquired pain
More broken parts, more second starts
More drugs, more shrunken veins

I will forget, but not forgive
Mercy favors the bold
I will regret the best I give
As Midas turning flesh to gold

I've given all the good I have
You never gave me much to start
So smile wide to mock their pride
It's hard to love a broken heart

Death of a Poet

The war is never won by lovers' rules
A battle cry in broken-hearted tune
Like Freyr gave his sword, immortal proof
Don't ask me to betray revenge so soon

O joy of feasting and of fighting long
The hand of violence, puppeting my heart
A brutal strength that only lovers know
I'll never ask the gods to do my part

To die in battle is Valhalla's gate
Your glory violence, not the victory
For righteous anger drips from moral hate
And death is not the worst of mortal schemes

My truest dreams are not on blood-soaked hills
I do not need to heal from lesser harms
Promise that you will stay while I am still
And I will starve to death wrapped in your arms

The Condemned Man's Lullaby

Maybe god is a biker
A little too tall and a little too bent
Struttin' around in bootcut jeans
And chuggin' on a cigarette

Maybe god is a railway car
Parked in a foreign port
Grafitti bloomin' on it's side
Life is a team sport

And maybe god is a runaway girl
Ridin' on the final train
And maybe god is my Nana's ghost
Singin' me to sleep again

Maybe god is a suicide pact
Or the one who tried to cheat
Said "You go first" and watched them die
And now he still can't sleep

Maybe god is a father's love
A face betrayed by age
But a steady hand and a steady gait
And a steady, patient gaze

And maybe god is a trickster boy
Spinnin' fate in a silken spiral
And maybe god is a battle corpse
Scattered on a funeral pyre

Maybe god is an immegrant
Workin' days for fifty cents
Watin' for his wife and kids
Smokin' butts for lunch to pay his rent

Maybe god is a scarecrow
Tied to a wooden pole
A sentinel of nightmares
Guardin' corn from the theivin' crows

Maybe god is a beautiful girl
Smilin' from across a room
Maybe god is an astronaut
Sailin' to a world new

Maybe god is a cryptid
Always rumored and never proved
Soon enough he'll leave us
Never carin' if we knew the truth

Maybe god is a homeless guy
Scrawling cocaine pencil art
And maybe god is a city cop
Tryin' hard to do her part

Maybe god is a Tuesday night
Cryin' in the toilet swirl
And maybe god killed his own child
And still couldn't save the world

Maybe god's each one of us
Maybe god's none at all
But maybe it doesn't matter much
'Till you've no one left to call

Forsake

Forsake me- I'm a lonely man
I take delight in my own plans
Spine and skull and teeth and bone
Revive the dream that time had stole
Spin the web of fate by hand
And mercifully loose my soul

Forsake me- solitary here
Living well beside my fears
Wond'rous wonton wanting more
Deep desire's dark downpour
Fetid flesh suprising steers
To places you have been before

Forsake me- most already gone
My silent solitude near won
At last remember where I go
Gentle grace from pain bestowed
Before the gods beheld the sun
I traced the waters far below

Forsake me- I must bear this joy
Awake at dawn once more a boy
To walk this world until it's done
And then I finally can run
Away from all, the cruel and coy
O won't the silence be so fun

Forsake me- now the night has come
The truth can't be contained in sum
Yet in this dark all else roams free
The comely lies of memory
Sweet forgotten darling son
It is not always good to see

Jawbone

I was wandering in the woods
Till something called my name
A deer, just under where I stood
Was missing half it's face
He looked at me with vacant eyes
And took a ragged breath
I pulled my pistol from my coat
Some wounds are only healed with death

I put my hand upon his head
And murmured to the sky
I don't know if you're up there
But another of your sons must die
You can hold this against me
When I am also cold and still
But since your mercy isn't here
To end his pain, I will

A moment more I hesitate
I feel him shivering with fear
And in the pregnant silence
Falls a single shimmering tear
A bullet cracks the quiet night
Across the leaves a smear of blood
I cannot feel my arms or legs
They drag me back into the woods

I don't remember walking home
I'm hurt in ways this world can't mend
So if you find me in the woods
I ask your mercy for my end

Holy Grail

Did it hurt when you fell from a fairy tale?
Dropped like snow and hit like hail
Rode a rainbow on a rail
To take your case to God

Did you fall apart in the evening
When the days were far too dark
You were busy in the woods that winter
When the journey home felt too far

Did you let me leave in silence
After living through the war
I wonder what you wanted now
And what you had needed before

Did it hurt when you drank from a holy grail?
Smelled like spit and hit like ale
Finally checked your brother's mail
And lost your faith in God

Garden

Sing to your sorrow
Give voice to your pain
You might be suprised
By all that remains
You'll never get better
While playing their games
The greatest things built
In the smallest of ways

Let go of your love and
Give wings to your heart
A few of us more than
The sum of our parts
With summertime sunder
Your soul into shards
The setting sun's plunder
A changing of guards

Wander the forest
Get lost from your head
Give ear to the secrets
Of wilds untread
Where nobody needs you
Go follow your breath
We all get an ending
The justice of death

Don't bury my body
In some sterile place
Let maggots and mushrooms
Grow out of my face
Roses and raspberries
Bloom from my chest
Tending this garden
I'll finally rest

III.

<u>Somewhere In Between</u>

Flight

What magic might have happened
On the nights we didn't spend
What hidden, precious secrets sleep
In words we never said
Each moment I am disappearing
Each moment I can't help from hearing
The quiet dreams and thoughts that words
Can never hope to touch

And so I drag my aching bones
From bed to face the moon
And so my restless mind scawls
Endless words in hope of song
And so my feet may wander, dear
I promise I'll not leave you here
I broke my heart so it could stay
From you, I only ask as much

Freedom is a lonely thing
I never liked the cold
Yet staying brings a heat
I cannot bear as I grow old

What beauty ever do I miss
When sleep takes me again
My legs will run away from me
If I don't soon give in
I lie each night upon my bed
And fear the day's first light
The awesome march of time treads on
And just as twilight dies to dawn
Before the loss of love and life lays low
I must take flight

Early Morning

As I awake to songbirds' cries
Upon a morning pleasant, bright and cool
The first thoughts of the day arise
And I am left again to choose
The careful reason of the wise
Or brilliant passion of the fool

Captain James Hook

I found the second star at last
And chased it to the dawn
But when I crashed upon that shore
My innocence was gone

I woke, half-buried in the sand
Lost Boy, it felt like grace
A Lost Man grew in Neverland
Killed me and took my place

The month I grew out of my shoes
And first I shaved my lip
I left to lead a pirate's life
Upon a pirate's ship

But soon I grew out of my boots
My crew abandoned me
I'll find the dread sirens' lagoon
And die in ecstacy

Working Class

You'll never work a day, they say
If you but love your trade
Would Satan really want to win
If Hell is his escape
Every time your eyes meet mine
My sanity is frayed
And if I want to be with you
Then first our children must be saved

A lonesome way to be awake
When all the world's asleep
But lonesome isn't loneliness
And I have secrets left to keep
The kings have rarely fought their wars
As David damned Uriah without grief
And subtlety is often nameless death
For those condemned by cruel beliefs

Barstools

Parasitic
Triple Sec
Symbiotic
Bite my neck

The night is almost over
But I won't end it sober
I'll be here a little longer
Unless offered something stronger

Quick lips
Soft thought
Long sips
Strong draught

The night is almost over
But I won't end it sober
Stay with me and call it sorrow
I'll be gone for good tomorrow

Regret
Move on
Forget
You're gone

The night is never over
And I won't end it sober
Light a pipe and fill a glass
Burn away my life at last

Lonely in a
Crowded room
Only sin and
Light perfume

And now the night is over
Again I wake up sober
Our pain between as common ground
If you had wanted to be found
I guess you would have stuck around
So I strike out for the next town
To find another drink to drown
All the hollow pain and sound
'Cause night is never over
And I still can't sleep sober

Alchemist

I keep a beaker 'neath the sink
To tally all my secret sins
There is no rush for me to fill
For soon I must partake again

First, comes wormwood, for to burn
The evil from my naked soul
Second, add a single leaf
Of hemlock to my beaker, whole

For each unforgivable sin
Douse in a drop of cyanide
Until the day my beaker fills
And then I must decide to die

Every change requires death
Each goal requires sacrifice
A choice is made, so be the one
To look and see the asking price

For long ago, there was a choice
Abundantly both plain and clear
I did not want to make a change
And now I pay the price of fear

Spit

Ever wonder what your mouth tastes like?

Spit

And a hint of regret.

Jezebel

O, my dearest Jezebel
        You've left me again
We were dancing in circles
        Outside in the rain
We didn't form words
        But our feet were ablaze
I held to your hands
        Found your eyes in the haze
And my footing was sure
        As we splashed through the pain

O, my dreadful Jezebel
        You've given my heart
A hope and a pernicious
        Muse to my art
If you take my hand
        Just know what you want
Poor Cupid's no lover
        He'll beat you at darts
I won't say I'm easy
        But at least I'm not smart
Don't give me a chance
        If you don't want my part

O, my lovely Jezebel
        Your passionate breath
Is my sleep and my reason
        To set aside death
Your kisses my food, dear
        Your beauty of myths
Your cruel lovemaking
        Is all I have left
You make me a fool
        And I play my part best
A lover not Heaven
        Nor Hell shall give rest

Run Away

Did you ever run away in the dead of night
Just to prove to them you'd make it out there
Watch all their pity dissolve into spite
When hunger drew you back to live in fear

Now you still forget to eat sometimes, until I come home

<><><>

The next time you ran away was in your first apartment
You never left the floor that night
Huddled alone in the kitchen corner
Trying to block out the voices of your parents
Calling you worthless

Now your blood has evaporated from the old wood floor
But you still can't wash the scars away

<><><>

The third time you ran away, it was open roads
Just you, the midnight radio, and an old minivan
But all things new must end again
Now we have tea parties and picnics
In your dear old friend, that yellow van
Every time it rains

<><><>

I know you want to run again
But if I can say one thing, my dear

Stay a moment here with me
We mustn't always be running
For I cannot dream
Without you in my arms

A Travelling Song

You had four years of college to finish
But the road, she was callin' my name
I'd say wait for me there, but it wouldn't be fair
I don't think I'll be waiting again

We called every day for the first month
Then suddenly weeks slipped away
But the lights of the city can't keep my mind busy
And I knew that I still couldn't stay

It's been only two years since I seen you
No, it doesn't feel like yesterday
So you gave up your jokes and I gave up the smokes
Nothin' ever stays quite the same way

◇◇◇

Sometimes I question my wandering mind
And wonder what goads me to roam
But it quickly comes clear when I ponder and peer
To be free, I can never be home

They say nothin' can ever be perfect
It's a concept that drives me insane
But we had it perfect, dear, for a brief time here
Each friend has a place in the pain

It's been twenty-three years since I seen you
And it feels now just like yesterday
As my mind burns with dreams, the distilled memories
Nothin' ever stays quite the same way

◇◇◇

I met god on a desolate mountain
I found peace on the endless black sea
I know hunger and death, just as close as my breath
Just as simple as you once knew me

I've done things that I never imagined
And I've done so much less than I hoped
But I feel it is time for my final goodbye
As I long once again for the road

It's been seventy years since I seen you
Some nights you still keep me awake
I told one of your jokes as I lit up my smoke
I guess some things are always the same

A Bit of Him

Pierce the darkness with a pin
And sew it up into a coat
Speckle stars across the fringe
A camouflage of half-dead hopes

Fasten clasp of lunar phase
And stride unseen into the night
To while away my youthful days
Slow dancing under traffic lights

I left a home I'd never known
Forgot to bring myself
I'm packing up my new wardrobe
When will I ask for help?

My stranger demons ponder wrongs
I can no longer boast
I do not wish to wander on
Unhaunted by your ghost

I am caretaker of this flesh
A vessel flung from birth to death
For him, I ever try to catch
A peaceful thought or pleasant breath

Daydream IV: Dad Shoes

You and your dad shoes
I remember them well
I worried you'd slip
While looking for shells

Dirt stained and creased
Walking out by the sea
I love those old dad shoes
'Cause they brought you to me

Daydream III: Lovely

Splash o' honey
Coffee cream
Eggs all runny
Pipe a'steam

Sitting empty
Empty house
Quiet plenty
Drying out

Smile softly
Cool dawn air
Softly falling
Damaged care

Caring less and
Loving more
Tell the future
Petrichor

Strength to pull me out of bed
Love to stay with me
Resting your chin on my head
A lovely morning dream

Seasons

◇WINTER◇

Down the frozen river trudge
The dreams of better men
My thoughts refuse to even budge
I'll leave them if I can
Until the water thaws with blood
I'll hide the bodies in the mud
By sacrifice appease the flood
Or is it all met out by chance

◇SPRING◇

Round the rowdy Maypole dance
My children wild and free
My husband sings as if entranced
By forest luxery
The stars come out and on we run
The moon intoxicates our fun
I'm howling like a loaded gun
In joyful madness find your peace

◇SUMMER◇

Lying in the river bed
The driest day in years
Spark the stars above my head
Illuminated tears
Burning thirst about me swirls
Shattered marbles made of pearl
Shining eyes and tangled curls
My sadness used to be so clear

◇AUTUMN◇

Hid among the ancient trees
A girl sleeps alone
She's bruised and bloody at the knees
She doesn't have a home
Yet in the dark she will be found
My children watch without a sound
I carry her through leafy bows
To set her broken bones

A Romance of Shadows

I feel the darkness in you darling
A deepest black of living blind
The same shadow I've thrown for years
You and I, a different kind

A padded world of pure white walls
Where no one wants you but for sport
I want to know your sickest thoughts
And feel your anger in retort

I'll find my passion in your eyes
Drink sadness from your lips
I'll bind my lust to love your body
Swing romance from your hips

My mind has wandered far and wide
My body clawed from hell
My spirit washed out in the tide
My soul an empty well

I want to know you better darling
Taste and listen, touch and see
I know we have a lot of choices
But for a while could we let this be?

A Small Brown Spider

It's quiet here
A bit too warm
A mile down the railroad bed

I have not seen
A single soul
The trains have long been dead

A spider wanders
Up my leg
I gently brush her off

And whisper softly
Sorry friend
I'll only get you lost

Autumn Death

A promise here of things to come
Good or bad I do not know
I am not who I thought I was
For that was many years ago

A whispered word of leafy breath
A garden laid to rest again
And with the autumn comes my death
The painted woods my best of friends

When autumn falls, I need no love
Before the winter cold has won
My afterlife in boughs above
To sway and watch the setting sun

To wander craggy mountain sides
On peaks that pierce the sky
In forests deeps is where I'll hide
And sing the stars alive

Soon, We're Going Sailing, Brother

Soon, we're going sailing, brother
Soon enough we go
Wandering the world, brother
More and more to know

Soon, we're going sailing, brother
Out to face ourselves
We're laughing and we're wailing, brother
Keep a steady helm

Soon, we're going sailing, brother
Won't return the same
The ocean she will change us, brother
Out beyond the bay

Soon, we're going sailing, brother
Sea to plastic sea
What will you be chasing, brother
When we can be free?

Soon, we're going sailing, brother
Leave memories behind
Our past it will not shape us, brother
Let the people die
The wild wind will chase us, brother
No one says goodbye

Funny

Where's the funny part in this?
You're laughing with your hands clenched into fists
Love, did you lose your way again?
You're shaking pretty hard after a night of sin

Why do you peddle your fragile soul
As if no one would give you what you need
Love, the living takes a toll
You never got enough for all you bleed

Sometimes we're given more than we can give
But no one's given more than they can take
Good things end where envy comes to live
Good intentions are easy to fake

Only true dispair remains inert
Someday there will be nothing to forget
What is it really worth if you can't get hurt?
Does rememberance ever come without regret?

Where's the funny part in this?
I'm laughing as my heart becomes remiss
Love, did you lose your way again?
You always used to find me after nightly sins

Darkness Dawning

What hath the wicked world wrought
This feeling in my bones
A sickness like the worst I've caught
Upon the wind has blown
Ignoring all that I've been taught
A fever to atone

Sharp words and sharper nails tease pain
On sallow sickly skin
A solemn kindness in the rain
A radiance within
We all must rest, he whispered small
Once we are free of sin

I came here small and screaming
And I'll leave the very same
I could listen to her breathing
More than Scripture any day
As my debts pile to the ceiling
I might not have long to stay

She held him down, but she could see
She couldn't keep him trapped
My freedom found beneath her weight
My best decisions mapped
Between her thighs, but in her eyes
Is where my strength is sapped

No Sodomite dares to invite
My wickedness upon
This curs`ed night of living right
Before the break of dawn
The wild call of darkness rings
Speak now before I'm gone

I won't accept a cautious love
So save yourself the wait
I ask her not to follow me
She knows I cannot stay
I'm going somewhere dangerous
To face these living pains

A Brief Lament

Don't you know you can't offend
A hopeless kind of heart
Starving under this pretense
Of knowing from the start
Ignoring obvious intent
To keep you in your part

Dying faster every day
Surviving more than fair
Lying mastered, naught to say
Defying shouted prayers
Mix the plaster, hide the cracks
Don't stay unless you dare
To look me in the eyes and see
The worst that lives in there

Contaminated pain relief
I'm drowning to escape
I surface to convince myself
This life ain't worth the weight
The stars a sharp and sweet motif
Maybe tonight I'll be alright
I'll keep it simple, short and sweet
It would be nice to share the wait

Tapping

That tapping that you hear, my dear
It's only in your head, my dear
Please lay back down to bed, my dear
I'm making sure that I'm still here

That ticking in your mind, my dear
The whispered scrape of wind, my dear
My unforgiven sin, my dear
Don't give your voice unto the fear

That tapping that you hear, my dear
It's all inside my head, my dear
Please lay back down to bed, my dear
I'm making sure that I'm still here

That ticking in your brain, my dear
My neverending pain, my dear
My mark a scarlet stain, my dear
A shame that angels cannot bear

That tapping that you hear, my dear
It's I alone in bed, my dear
Please rest your pretty head, my dear
I'm making sure that I'm still here

Sailing

Earth birthed us
Gods shape us
What's worth this?
Love breaks us
Hate burns us
Shame takes us
Joy sells us
We make us
Your hell's kiss
My statements
All selfish
All reckless

No anchor
No sail
No rudder to steer
Full tankard
At full mast
A sea full of fears
Pour out the tankard
And fill it with tears
And scream at the stars
Beyond angels' ears
Where no one will hear

Kissing

Kissing cigarettes
Against my stone cold lips
Breath in and forget
Your hungry, restless hips
Hazy eyes, the taste of smoke
Dazed and crying, save your hope
Choke me out and swallow spit
The dying ain't the worst of it

Kissing bloody earth
The lucky ones all died
What is heaven worth
When you are on the other side
There's always a temptation, love
And anger only needs a shove
Everyone must take a side
A reckless love you cannot buy

Kissing bottled death
This smell is getting old
Reminder of your breath
So measured in the cold
I saw you in an angel choir
Before I lit the house on fire
I will not join you on the road
The living isn't what we're told

Finally kissed your lips
Your tongue tasted like wine
Wind is pushing south
A call that isn't mine
I never have been one to follow
Our silence doesn't seem so hollow
Don't know where I'll be tomorrow
Love, it takes a bit of time

Road Trips and Song Skips

Her room's a mess; she says she's on the mend
I go outside to burn a pack of cigarettes
If you can't take this life just make pretend
Hope kills more than it saves in the end

My dreams won't let me sleep late anymore
I shiver as my feet hit the cold floor
She calls me back to bed, but I'm already out the door
There's ghosts inside that house I can't ignore

She found me in my car beside the road
Grabbed my hand and said We've got to go
Darling don't you get it? How to run is all I know
And I'll take you as far as you will go

I think I sobered up a little bit
The day she rolled the car into a ditch
Can almost bear to see her leave, I can't to see her quit
Before I give my heart, I lose my wits

I dropped her at the door to catch a plane
I never liked the airport, can't explain
She's going home for Christmas, but I'm driving on again
I can't stop or I think I'll go insane

Got back from my Americana tour
When I last saw her, her black hair was short
Now it's long and tangled, nothing like it was before
I don't know what to do with you no more

Home

Con men selling false religion
From a dead payphone
Lonely poets lie together
Under leagues of stone
Faithful soldiers bathed in blood
Rendered still and prone
And it's never really worth it
Until someone calls you home

Piercing look across a room
Left me wanting more
Quiet contemplation stolen
On a foreign shore
Forged in flesh and birthed from bone
And justified in gore
And after mammon doesn't matter
Who will be the poor?

Shudder with the galaxies
And barter with the crones
Give the kings electric chairs
And give the homeless thrones
The whisper of the orphan queen
Drowns out entitled moans
And it's never really worth it
Until someone calls you home

Living large and fading fast
Hunger ain't hard to please
But feed the lips of discontent
Find longing company
A scarlet rope around my neck
To save my dignity
It grates on me to stay one place
Be lonely, wild and free

Sail again to world's end
Along the faceless foam
Follow trail by tooth and nail
Or make your way alone
Let your body wander wide
And forge a heart of stone
But it's never really worth it
Until someone calls you home

Chant

When all of the smoke has dried out my eyes
So I can't even try to cry
I just want to know I'm real

When all of my debts are lost in the fire
My sanity stretched like a wire
I just want to know I'm real

When all of your love is for somebody else
No, I don't really want your help
I just want to know that I'm real

And when all of the birds begin singing again
After picking us clean of our sin
I just want to know that I'm real

When all of the money can't buy you forgiveness
And you still dare to call yourself sinless
I just want to know that I'm real

When all of the laughter of children is rotten
And no one quite wants what we've gotten
I just want to know that I'm real

When all of the sadness has stopped me from crying
Bitterness has stopped me from trying
I just want to know that I'm real

When all of your joy is with somebody else
And I see that you're happy and free
I just want to know that I'm real

When you promise your heart to the one that you love
And you finally don't need to have me
I just want to know that I'm real

When we've all played our parts and the theatre is done
And we've spun out our time with the sun
I just want to know that I'm real

When nobody's there when you crawl to the shore
And you can't feel your legs from the cold
I just want to know that I'm real

And would anyone care when I've said my last words
To remember me after I'm gone
I just want to know that I'm real

Just One More Drive

Just one more drive and then I'm home
And you'll no longer be alone
I'm losing all my sense of place
And getting in a bad head space
When I ain't on the open road
Just one more drive and then I'm home

Just one more walk among the trees
To brush my hands against the leaves
To dip my head into the pond
Perhaps you'd think to come along
Climb a pine and feel the breeze
Just one more walk among the trees

Just one more weekend in a tent
Boundless nature still unfenced
Before I drag my feet back home
Out here you might feel less alone
To watch the night sky from your bed
Just one more weekend in a tent

Just one more climb atop the roof
And I will no more ask for proof
To stop out on a lonely road
And watch the autumn stars unfold
Howlin' ballads like a wolf
Just one more climb atop the roof

Lover, Sinner, Dancer, Brother, Sister

O Lover, you are gone from me now
And when I find you there I'll lay me down
The spring's first kiss greets me soft in the evening
A gentle scent of childhood and rain
And in my reckless mind and hopeless dreaming
My memories are locked away again

<><><>

O Sinner, you have made my path so long
Your music worms its way into my chest
You satisfied my hunger with your song
I'll satisfy your hunger with my flesh
I don't ask much before your task is through
I have to kiss the bottle before you

<><><>

O Dancer, on the day you left my side
I knew at once that everyone must die
I kept my ego, but you took my pride
I dreamed you as a brilliant star of fire
You burned away my fear and my desire
And scarred your flaming visage in my eyes

<><><>

O Brother, you will never be alone
I know it's awful hard to make a home
And on the days you wish you weren't alive
I'll find my way to you and stay beside
Our brotherhood a promise, blood in hand
And someday we might find the promised land

<><><>

O Sister, you were there to see me cry
You held my hand in darkness on the night
When everybody else left me to die
You left me words along my path as lights
I'll meet you one more time before the end
We'll laugh and sing under the stars again

Making Friends

Making friends with the cracks in your ceiling and floor
Running behind
Killing our time
Making friends with the tomcat who waits at your door
Never you mind
Innocent crime

Making friends with the cracks in your face and your hands
Homesick again
Touching your skin
Making friends with the names buried under the sand
Not knowing when
Moments begin

Making friends with the ravens who habit this place
Secretive lore
Festivities
Making friends with an angel who's fallen from grace
Holistic cure
Climbing in trees

Making friends with the demons trapped inside your eyes
Ultimate price
Matter of pride
Making friends with the scars on my wrists and my thighs
Virtue or vice
Vacant divide

Another Song

I met her in the morning light
I was wasted on the road
She took pity on my form
And brought my body home
I've waited for her patiently
But I won't wait too long
I've got to get out 'fore she comes
And write just one more song

Could you dare imagine it
A pool deep in the woods
Yet undefiled by mankind
With water sweet and good
Don't ask me, for I do not have
A home where I belong
Go find yourself a warmer place
And leave me to my song

I cannot read the hearts of men
They're simple but confused
I tried to tell her what I want
She left me no excuse
I tried to hold my anger but
She never did me wrong
I think I lost my way a'lookin'
For another song

I ain't been here for much time
And I won't be here much more
I've seen a million starving souls
Ride that revolving door
When I hear that angel knock
On heaven's gaudy gong
Tell god he cannot have me yet
I've still got one more song

I met her once upon the day
I left my mother's womb
I'll meet her one more time upon
The threshold of my tomb
Don't try to outrun her embrace
You'll never be that strong
Sweet Death will be my lover soon
Just give me one more song

Far Far Down Below

Far far down below
Shivering through the gates
Down beneath the broken teeth
And tongues that whisper fate
Dance on down to my home town
If you're bent to bet on hate
Suckle near on lips of tears
To bear the deathless wait

Far far down below
Spasmed sounds of song
Cindered lungs are naked hung
From branches young and strong
Upon a steed of hungry need
My daughters punish wrong
Perfect the sham of honest man
Eyes wriggling along

Far far down below
Caked in lonely scorn
Silver pail for catching hail
A god has been still-born
Insipid shock the only clock
That governs eve or morn
Fit punishment for asking rent
To sound the iron horn

Far far down below
Aware of creeping dread
The reaper birds trail listless words
To set heaven to bed
A gruesome cry defiles the sky
Of vengeance yet unfed
Will no one loose the orphan's noose
The clergy want him dead

Far far down below
Beyond the sight of gods
A seizured brain of sparkling pain
Puts poetry to thought
A broken home ain't built alone
What hath unkindness wrought
No mortal name remains the same
Some ways remain untrod

Far far down below
Mistreated children grown
Remember joys of rhythmic noise
As preachermen are stoned
The poisoned dream of apathy
Scattered among the bones
For even weeds have little needs
And much is left unknown

Rain

The best kind of songs make me feel things
You made me feel nothing but pain
I guess I should have left you strung out
In the backseat of your car out in the rain

No one ever came to save me from my anger
No Messiah found me and I won't be yours
Left your name under a stone somewhere in Vermont
It will be there for you when I depart your door

I copied an eight-track of all of the songs
I will never partake of again
Wrote your name on the back, threw it into the pond
And walked home alone in the rain

Our time is so short that I must tarry long
In places I shouldn't exist
Like the piece of my heart buried under the pond
Or the only time we ever kissed

Christmas

Leaky windows dripping carols
Under Christmas lights
Creaky hinges, doorway sterile
Digging graves tonight

Kissing warmth into my fingers
Under mistletoe
Mourning chill about me lingers
Trudging through the snow

Leaky boots, winter's first chill
A simple evergreen
Weakly smile and climb the hill
Of Christmas memories

Flirt

Don't mistake my attention for romance
Don't let innocence go to waste
It's been a long time since I let myself love
You will not change that with such haste
My solitude is well-encased

I will not remember your caution
Your careful words will be forgot
Life is far too short for a measured report
Impermanence cannot be fought
The living with dying is fraught

I'm not too fond of quiet
But the silence I can stand
Don't touch me unless you are willing to follow
I've still got some blood on my hands
I've dug too many graves across these lands

My tea tastes burnt and bitter
And it's hot enough to hurt
Mama didn't raise a quitter
And if there's nothing after all but dirt
I cannot waste the time to stay and flirt

Revel

Everyone's got to revel in something
I never found it in a god
Got closer than I wanted this evening
And feeling a bit like a fraud
Some nights I still think that I'm teething
From headaches that strangle my sleep
The soup on the stove has been seething
To flavor the flesh as it steeps

Everyone's got to revel in something
I couldn't find it in your eyes
Warmed by the fire of a bush struck by lightning
Or a Bible, a match, and a lie
I coughed up a stone that was jagged and shining
The sum of my meaningless art
And I couldn't place that sensation of pining
Till you told me the stone was my heart

Everyone's got to revel in something
Escape is a felony charge
You keep yourself busy with goings and comings
I'm walking the path to the stars
An old wooded road with the little frogs peeping
A stairway cutting through the rain
If you're lucky enough you just might hear them singing
The ghosts of the ramblers' train

Printed in the United States
by Baker & Taylor Publisher Services